The Mentor's Guide

Therapeutic Riding Instructor—
Registered Level

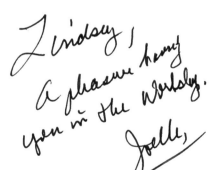

Joelle M. Devlin

PATH Intl Master Instructor

PATH Intl Lead Evaluator—Registered, Advanced and Master Instructor
Certification Levels

© 2015 Joelle M. Devlin

All Rights Reserved.

No part of this publication may be reproduced, stored in a retrieval system, or transmitted, in any form or by any means, electronic, mechanical, photocopying, recording, or otherwise, without the written permission of the author.

First published by Dog Ear Publishing
4011 Vincennes Rd
Indianapolis, IN 46268
www.dogearpublishing.net

ISBN: 978-1-4575-3853-7

This book is printed on acid-free paper.

Printed in the United States of America

ACKNOWLEDGMENTS

The future of the EAAT industry is dependent upon new instructors coming into the field. The better educated and skilled these instructors are, the more benefit our riders around the world will receive. These newcomers are dependent upon skilled and knowledgeable mentors to lead the way. With that in mind, the following colleagues very generously offered their time and expertise to review *The Mentor's Guide* at various stages in its development.

Enormous thanks are due to Sue Adams, who contributed so greatly to the first draft of this guide. It was she who suggested the WHAT/HOW/WHY format that gives the book its structure. Many thanks to Sandy Webster for so graciously reviewing and editing the *entire* first draft of this workbook. As always, her kind and knowledgeable notes were much appreciated. Also thanks to Marsha Anderson, who gave her time to review that fledgling version. And thanks to Shayna Bolton for suggesting we add forms and checklists to make it more user-friendly. One of the wonderful things about this industry is peer support. Value it and use it!!

Contents

INTRODUCTION

Congratulations on your decision to become a mentor to Therapeutic Riding Instructors! It can be a fun, exciting venture with great rewards—for your trainees, for you as a mentor, as well as for the Therapeutic Riding Industry as a whole. By bringing new TR Instructors into the fold, you are creating the future of the industry.

The objective of this workbook is to help you to be the best mentor you can be. Having mentored numerous would-be Therapeutic Riding Instructors over the years, we've learned a few things that may be of help to you. Here are a few tips, just to begin:

1)   No two trainees are alike.

As mentors, we are training adults, guiding them, preparing them for a new career path. They each bring with them a past—certain skills and abilities, possibly even talents; areas of knowledge; individual methods of learning; processing time; work ethic; and a life that may or may not accommodate your training schedule. They have differing levels of self-confidence and hopefully, a passion for Therapeutic Riding. Last but not least, they will each have a very individual sense of humor. Exploring these traits and establishing mutual expectations before agreeing to accept the role of mentor can alleviate misconceptions and conflict down the road and lead to a successful relationship.

Once a plan is agreed upon, discovering how best to guide each individual to success is the meat of successful mentoring.

2) If you are mentoring to "pass a test," the results will *not* be satisfactory.

When training is conducted simply to pass a test, there is typically a strict deadline established and training is focused on those elements that are defined as "required." On the other hand, if we commit to mentor an instructor-in-training to become an effective Therapeutic Riding Instructor, we open the potential for acceptance of far more information and establish a relationship that is richer, with a far deeper exchange of knowledge. **The trainee's focus then shifts to learning <u>how to benefit their riders</u> rather than passing a test.** A truly effective Therapeutic Riding Instructor with solid skills should be able to pass any test.

3) If you're not having fun, neither are they.

Therapeutic Riding is a serious business. We accept responsibility for putting people of all ages with varying levels of abilities on the back of a horse. This is a high-risk activity. On the other hand, having fun is a very important aspect of TR. It is simply *more fun* than going to a clinic or a therapist's office. We want our lessons to be enjoyable for riders, volunteers, as well as instructors. A trainee should also enjoy the learning process. If not, the students they teach during their practicum will miss out on this very important quality.

With all of that in mind, this workbook has been designed as a guide to assist a mentor in covering the essential information while building a relationship of trust and support with the trainee—and having fun in the process of sharing their knowledge. It discusses the following:

WHAT   What are the essential areas of knowledge needed to be an effective Therapeutic Riding Instructor?

WHY   Why is each of these topics essential?

HOW   How can the information best be presented to an instructor-in-training (including ways to have fun while imparting your wisdom)?

This is not a textbook. It does not presume to offer all of the knowledge needed to effectively train a Therapeutic Riding Instructor. For each topic, references are given to enable more in-depth study and education. It is a succinct guide to assist a mentor in the planning and execution of a training program. We hope you find it helpful as you enrich the industry by guiding new talent to become effective Therapeutic Riding Instructors.

1

THE MENTOR

Characteristics of a Good Mentor

A mentor is:

- **A wise and trusted counselor or teacher, an influential senior sponsor or supporter** (Dictionary.com).

- **An experienced and trusted advisor** (Google.com).

- **One who imparts wisdom, expands vision, and shares knowledge with a less experienced colleague** (Wikipedia).

I. First and foremost, a mentor must have an interest in helping others to reach their potential, to be successful. To do so, **honest self-assessment** is critical. A mentor must have sufficient knowledge to impart to the trainee to guide them to success. In Therapeutic Riding, this would require in-depth knowledge in the following areas:

- Horses and horsemanship

- Disabilities

- The relationship between the two

- PATH INTL Certification Criteria

- PATH INTL Certification Process

- PATH INTL Standards

Recognizing that we all have strengths and weaknesses—no one knows it all—having a list of sources of information, as well as others who can supplement knowledge in each of these areas, can be very helpful. Any means of encouraging growth and knowledge for the mentor as well as the trainee is of value.

II. In the same vein, a good mentor must be committed to **lifelong learning.** Being open to learn, even from our trainees, and seeking out new knowledge is essential in this business. The more we know, the more we have to offer our riders and trainees.

III. A mentor must be **willing to commit his or her time** to the instructor-in-training. Being available to discuss ideas and to support the trainee in their journey can be one of the most difficult aspects of mentoring, but it is also one of the most important and the most rewarding.

IV. A good mentor is **always positive, always supportive, and always ready to listen, to observe, and to offer ideas/solutions** to issues as they arise for the trainee. Learning is a journey. It will have its challenges. The mentor's role is to guide the trainee over those hurdles, always offering support and belief in the trainee's ability to succeed.

Taking on the role of a mentor is a great responsibility. It's a role that can be very rewarding when a **positive, professional relationship is maintained**. This workbook has been designed to offer the **WHATs/HOWs/WHYs** of each essential topic to be covered, with suggestions on how to guide both you and your trainee to enjoy a positive and successful experience while preparing them to enter the fascinating field of TR.

WHAT   PATH Intl REGISTERED LEVEL CRITERIA

WHY   PATH Intl sets the standards for therapeutic riding. The criteria published in their application booklet defines those skills the organization feels are essential for a therapeutic riding instructor to be effective. These are the standards PATH evaluators will use when determining whether a candidate has sufficient skills to be awarded PATH Registered Level Riding Instructor Certification. By referring to the criteria as the basis for training, mentoring goes beyond personal opinion to apply professional, objective standards.

HOW   <u>Classroom</u>

- The listing of criteria found in the PATH Certification Application Booklet can be used as a checklist for self-assessment. The trainee/s can assess their own strengths and weaknesses at the beginning of the study period. This gives you as mentor a clear starting point for each individual, as well as the basis for a training plan. It will identify those areas that need the most work, as well as strengths to be built upon. It can be an objective tool for joint review throughout the training.

- Accurate self-assessment can be difficult. Utilizing video tapes or actual lessons being taught to demonstrate acceptable skill levels can be very helpful. Offering a running commentary on the demos and pointing out the strengths and weaknesses as they relate to the standards, will help to clarify. Keeping the assessments objective, based on the standards rather than your opinion alone, can help build trust between you and your trainee.

- To be effective and build trust, remember to place as much emphasis on the trainee's strengths as you do on their weaknesses. A good mentor encourages success. Look for the positives first and then correct the weaker areas.

Have fun   **If you are working with more than one instructor-in-training, it is likely that one will be weak where another is strong. Encouraging them to work together to support each other by sharing their talents, will make the training sessions more fun and create a bond that will last throughout their careers in therapeutic riding.**

Homework

The trainees should take the criteria home with them to review. This is not a project to be taken lightly or finished quickly. This will determine how their training will proceed. Give them time and encourage them to think it through in depth.

Reference:

PATH Intl, *Registered Certification Application Booklet.*

2

DISABILITIES

WHAT   DISABILITIES

WHY   The objective of every therapeutic riding lesson is to benefit the rider by improving their functional level. To provide safe and effective service, an instructor must have an understanding of the characteristics of their rider's disability, including potential precautions and contraindications, as well as how those characteristics may impact the student's style of learning and pace of progress.

It is the responsibility of a Therapeutic Riding Instructor to have sufficient knowledge to:

1) Determine if therapeutic riding is appropriate for a prospective rider;

2) Determine realistic goals and objectives for the rider;

3) Match horse to rider for the greatest benefit;

4) Assign appropriate tack;

5) Determine volunteer needs;

6) Determine appropriate mount and dismount techniques;

7) Determine which teaching techniques will be most effective;

8) Progress the rider at a realistic pace.

These responsibilities can be met only if the instructor has a working knowledge and understanding of the characteristics of the rider's disability. A review of basic anatomy and kinesiology will be helpful: The *Anatomy Coloring Book* is a great guide to help develop a basic understanding of the muscular, skeletal, and sensory systems of the human body.

HOW

Classroom

Review the files of each of the riders the trainee/s will be teaching, with particular emphasis on the Physician's Form. Have the trainee/s look up each disability in a medical dictionary and in PATH Intl Precautions and Contraindications. Next, review how the information will impact their plans for this student in relation to choice of horse, choice of mount/dismount, choice of tack, volunteer assignments, lesson objectives, teaching style, and finally any questions that need to be asked of the rider, their family, or their physician.

Have fun

Assign your trainee/s a disability to simulate - for example: hemiplegia, ADHD, using a blindfold for visual impairment or earplugs for hearing impairment, and so on. Then give them a riding lesson. It's a fun exercise that teaches empathy for the riders. The more they can feel what their riders feel, the more effective they will be as instructors.

Homework

Assign your trainee/s a disability to study in depth and report on. Using the Disability Study Guide on the next page, the report should include causes, characteristics, precautions and contraindications, potential for improvement, and how therapeutic riding can be of benefit. Next, have them write two or three consecutive lesson plans indicating how they would progress a rider with this disability. The lesson plan should include choice of horse, tack, mount/dismount, volunteer needs, and teaching techniques.

This can be done once to illustrate how to research a disability, or it can be a weekly project to add knowledge of multiple disabilities.

References:

PATH Intl Standards Manual. Precautions & Contraindications

Kapit, Wynn & Elson, Lawrence, *The Anatomy Coloring Book,* Pearson Education Limited, England, 2014.

Medical Dictionaries

Therapeutic Riding I & II Strategies for Instruction, 1998 ISBN 0-9633065-5-3, Editor Barbara T. Engel.

Disability Study Guide   Disability: _____

		Reference/s
Cause		
Characteristics		
Precautions & Contraindications		
Realistic Long-term Goals		
Applicable Riding Skills		
How TR Can Benefit This Rider		
Suggested Horse/Tack/Volunteer Needs		

WHAT   POSTURE & ALIGNMENT

WHY   Correct posture and alignment (an imaginary line from ear to shoulder to hip to the back of the heel and centered left to right) is essential for the security and effectiveness of any rider, but particularly for those with a disability. Only when the body is properly aligned can the rider follow the motion of the horse and receive the full benefit of the horse's movement. Developing an eye for posture and alignment and discovering the tools to make corrections in a riders' position will form the basis for effective instruction. Benefits include:

- Improved balance and mobility;

- Improved body awareness;

- Improved ability to follow the motion of the horse;

- Greater security in the saddle;

- Improved proprioceptive and vestibular input;

- Increased comfort of horse and rider;

- Tactful use of aids;

- Communication with the horse;

- Developing a functional base—the foundation of effective riding.

For those riders who cannot accomplish correct posture and alignment due to their disability, **approximation** is a most effective means of improving their functional level. In each lesson, corrections are made to come closer and closer to the ideal. Couple these corrections with the motion of the horse, and over time, you have the basis of what makes horseback riding therapeutic.

HOW   <u>Classroom</u>

- Review various positions of the pelvis—neutral; anterior/posterior tilt; lateral shift; full rotation; weight shift right; weight shift left. Having trainees demonstrate each of these positions and their impact on overall posture will help drive home the importance of first addressing the position of the pelvis in their riders and making corrections proximal to distal.

- The instructors-in-training can bring in video tapes or still shots of themselves riding and/or their students to review posture and alignment and discuss what corrections would be needed to improve their position. Check from the side as well as from the back. Reviewing terminology and phrasing that might be effective in making the corrections will give the trainee the tools they will need in the arena.

- Guide discussion on what impacts posture and alignment. This will offer the trainees a basis for horse/rider matching, as well as assist them with decisions to be made regarding tack and lesson activities.

    - Muscle tone

    - Range of Motion (ROM)

    - Sensory impairment

- Body types

- Conformation of horse and rider

- Choice of tack

- Tack fit and adjustment

- Type of motion of the horse

- Gait

- Lesson activities

- Others?

Have Fun: Have the trainee/s mount a horse and purposely ride with poor posture and alignment at walk and trot. This kinesthetic exercise will demonstrate more effectively than any words or pictures the impact poor posture and alignment will have on their riders. Have them describe how it feels, what part of the body is being stressed, and what correction is needed.

Homework

Trainees should observe riders in lessons, noting any improvements or the lack thereof in posture and alignment as the lesson progresses and why: What made the difference? How did the activities during the lesson affect change? What correction from the instructor was effective? What suggestions might they have to foster further improvement? How did posture and alignment impact the rider's performance?

References

Professional Association of Therapeutic Horsemanship International, *Instructor Educational Guide.*

Pony Club, *The Manual of Horsemanship*, International Printing House, Cairo, 1997.

Certified Horsemanship Association, *Horsemanship Manual*, 2008.

Therapeutic Riding I & II Strategies for Instruction, 1998 ISBN 0-9633065-5-3, Editor Barbara T. Engel.

WHAT   MOUNT/DISMOUNT

WHY

The mount and dismount are typically the most challenging parts of a therapeutic riding lesson. For the mount, the rider has not yet benefitted from the motion of the horse; the horse may have had a few minutes of warm- up, but he may not have proven himself in a lesson yet that day; the mounting block or ramp are not places of comfort for the horse; the mounting equipment presents a hazard should anything go wrong. Add to this a rider with cognitive or physical limitations, and the result is a situation that must be handled with skill and understanding, with *safety* for all participants as a primary consideration.

The mounting technique chosen will impact the performance of the rider throughout the class. The more independent the mount, the more independent the student will be in the lesson. The more successful the mount, the more relaxed the rider will be throughout the lesson.

A poorly executed dismount can eliminate any benefit the rider may have gained from his time in the saddle.

HOW

Classroom

Hands-on practice is required to learn the various mount and dismount techniques an instructor will need to accommodate a variety of disabilities. Use the attached checklist to be sure all are covered. These would include:

Mounts:	Croup mount	-	from block and ramp
	Crest mount	-	from block and ramp
	Two-man lift	-	from ramp
	Wheelchair transfer	-	from ramp
	Stand & pivot	-	from ramp
	Mechanical lift (if available)		from ramp

Dismounts:	Croup to ground/to wheelchair
	Crest and modified crest to ground/to wheelchair
	Two-man lift to wheelchair
	Emergency dismount techniques

While practicing the above techniques, it is important to keep in mind that safety and good time management during the mounting segment are dependent upon being organized and following a consistent system of steps including:

- Thorough tack check before entering block or ramp;

- Volunteers well-positioned and trained in their roles;

- Riders' helmets properly fitted;

- Horses warmed up, checked for soundness, and relaxed

- Mounting order determined.

Mount/dismount techniques should initially be practiced on a stabilized barrel or other stationary device that will allow simulation of the techniques without the use of an actual horse. This is both for the safety of all involved and to avoid unnecessary discomfort for the horse.

Once a sufficient level of skill is acquired, the trainee should progress to mounting progressively more involved riders with the mentor in position to assist if needed. Before each lesson, a thorough discussion of the planned technique should be scheduled with the trainee and the volunteer team.

Have fun   **The best way to learn a mount or dismount technique is to experience how the rider feels during its execution. Have your trainee/s simulate a variety of disabilities. Either fellow trainees or you as mentor will then mount and dismount using the various techniques listed above. You'll then change places to afford them hands-on practice. Again, this can be done on a stretching barrel or other stationary device to save the horses.**

Homework

Working with specific rider's characteristics, have trainees determine the following:

1) The factors that will determine mount/dismount techniques. These Include:

Student	Horse	Instructor	Volunteer	Facility
Height	Height	Height	Height	Equipment
Weight	Training	Training	Training	Tack
Skill level	Base	Skill level	Skill level	
Age	Age		Maturity	
Disability			Number	

2) Review PATH Intl standards regarding mounting, particularly regarding the mounting area and equipment to be used.

3) While maintaining the dignity of the student, the least restrictive environment that affords a safely executed mount/dismount should be chosen. To promote independence, every effort should be made to offer the rider as close to an able-bodied riding experience as possible within the parameters of safety.

4) Review good body mechanics while executing the mount and dismount to protect the instructor as well as the student.

5) Review the role of each member of the volunteer team in the different mount/dismount techniques. The instructor is responsible for guiding the entire team in the execution of a safe mount/dismount.

6) Review the order of mount/dismount and the factors that determine it: tone, stamina, stability, ability to wait, instructor attention needed, etc.

7) Review how to teach mount and dismount as a skill to both the rider and the volunteer team.

References:

Professional Association of Therapeutic Horsemanship International, *Instructor Educational Guide.*

Therapeutic Riding I & II Strategies for Instruction, 1998 ISBN 0-9633065-5-3, Editor Barbara T. Engel.

Mount/Dismount Checklist   Name:

		Intro	Practice	Accomplished
MOUNTS				
Croup	Block			
	Ramp			
Crest	Block			
	Ramp			
Wheelchair Transfer	Ramp			
Stand & pivot	Ramp			
Two-man Lift	Ramp			
Mechanical Lift	Ramp			
DISMOUNTS				
Croup	To ground			
	To wheelchair			
Crest	To ground			
	To wheelchair			
Two-man lift	To wheelchair			
Emergency dismount techniques				

3

LESSON PLANS

WHAT   LESSON PLANS

WHY   To be effective, a Therapeutic Riding Instructor must be thoroughly pre-pared before entering the arena. Every minute of a lesson should be pur-poseful and meaningful for the riders. Each element requires thoughtful planning toward an objective to be truly of benefit.

Several skills are required in order to write a valid lesson plan:

- Establishing an appropriate and challenging **Objective**

- Defining the **Task Analysis** of the skill to be taught

- Establishing **Skill Progression**

- Creating **Progression Within the Lesson**

Each of these skills is significant and worthy of in-depth review. Each is individually addressed in the following pages.

WHAT   GOALS & OBJECTIVES

WHY   Each lesson taught should have a single **objective**—one riding skill the student/s will perform within that particular lesson. This gives the lesson focus for the rider/s, the instructor and the volunteers. Having a single objective allows the instructor to teach one riding skill in depth and see improvement within every lesson. Determining an appropriate objective requires review of the student/s' disabilities, as well as their long-term goals.

HOW   <u>Classroom</u>

Determining objectives can be best accomplished in three steps:

1. Determine **long-term goals**. These are typically goals the student or their caregiver/s will determine and are usually therapy goals: improved balance; improved gross/fine motor skills; improved speech; improved focus; etc. These goals can be accomplished through therapeutic riding over a period of time. It may take years, but this is the reason they have come to a therapeutic riding program.

2. Determine **short-term goals**. By breaking the long-term goals down into manageable segments, short-term goals can be determined. For example: Within the first year or the first session, what will be the focus? Which goal will be addressed, and what level of accomplishment in which riding skill will be expected? Perhaps to address fine motor skills little Mary will be expected to hold the reins consistently for an entire lesson, or will she be able to perform the posting trot independently by the end of the year?

3. Determine the **lesson objective**. If the short-term goal is posting trot by the end of a ten-week semester, what must be covered in week one to prepare the student to succeed in the skill by week ten? The objective for each lesson in the session will then build on the one before, providing progression within the session, always addressing the long-term goals.

The first step in writing effective lesson plans is to practice writing an **objective**. You can assign a riding skill or allow the trainee/s to determine it. The objective can be written for a rider they know or simply to practice structuring an objective properly. An objective must have the following three components:

1. An **action word** (*will post, will demonstrate, will maintain, will perform*, etc.)

2. A **horsemanship skill** (steering, posting, halting, backing/reinback, cantering/loping, etc.)

3. A **measureable component** (3 out of 5 attempts, from A to B, 50% of the lesson, etc.)

Objectives can also include levels of assistance as they relate to skill progression. A rider might accomplish the proper use of the reins with hand-over-hand assistance versus accomplishing it independently. They might sit the trot for the designated A to B using a handhold, or can they accomplish it without adaptive equipment? Do they require a leader and two side walkers or can they accomplish the objective skill with a spotter only?

The objective should focus on one riding skill to be accomplished in that lesson, and it should be stated with sufficient detail to allow a substitute instructor to follow it without additional information. If well-structured, it will keep the instructor focused and allow the review of rate of progression toward a goal by determining weekly successes.

Examples: Sally will demonstrate a consistent posting trot one full lap of the arena in each direction on the rail with spotter only.

Johnny will use both verbal and rein cues for whoa 3 out of 5 attempts with verbal prompts only.

Have fun   The trainees can write objectives for their own training. Let them determine their long-term goals. They can choose one, break it down into short-term goals, and then compose a series of progressive objectives for each study session. They may need some help determining the task analysis or steps along the way to accomplishing some of their goals, so be prepared. Applying the concept to their own learning can make the process far more meaningful.

Homework

Have the trainee/s observe riders, read their paperwork, and then review long- term goals—perhaps over the period of one year. Once a long-term goal has been discussed and accepted as realistic and appropriate, determine at what point the rider should be -by the end of the current semester. They will then write progressive objectives for each lesson within that semester. All objectives should lead to the pre-established semester goal.

References:

Professional Association of Therapeutic Horsemanship International, *Instructor Educational Guide.*

Pony Club, *The Manual of Horsemanship*, International Printing House, Cairo, 1997.

Therapeutic Riding I & II Strategies for Instruction, 1998 ISBN 0-9633065-5-3, Editor Barbara T. Engel.

WHAT   TASK ANALYSIS

WHY   Task analysis is the isolating, sequencing, and describing of the essential components of a task. For equestrian purposes, it is breaking down a horsemanship skill into multiple, sequential steps to be taught in a particular order.

This is the **HOW** of the lesson, the information the instructor will give to the students to guide them to successfully perform the skill being taught. This allows the students to learn, step-by-step, each component of the skill in a logical progression.

Analyzing a task allows an instructor to teach it in incremental steps. Breaking it down for the riders, particularly those with physical or learning disabilities, can mean the difference between failure and success. It also makes the instructor more aware of the almost-infinite number of accomplishments their riders will have to master before they can be successful in the overall task assigned. It can be the basis for progression of objectives from one lesson to the next, working together toward the goal.

Doing task analysis affords the instructor a very detailed understanding of each skill, allowing them to teach it in greater depth. It is a tool that will make the IT a far more conscious and effective instructor.

HOW   <u>Classroom</u>

- Each trainee should choose a riding skill and, using the Task Analysis Worksheet in this section, perform a task analysis of the skills needed to accomplish it correctly. Once they feel the analysis is complete, have them break down each of their preliminary steps into yet another level. Continue this process until they can go no further. Example:

<u>The halt</u>:

<u>Level 1</u>: 1) Sit deep; 2) Bring reins back; 3) Say whoa; 4) Release reins

<u>Level 2</u>: What skills or abilities are required to accomplish each of these steps correctly? Bringing reins back requires fine motor skills to hold the reins, upper trunk stability, sufficient ROM in the elbows and shoulders, as well as strength to bring them back toward the hip and the ability to judge how much pressure to exert, etc.

- Once you feel the tasks have been thoroughly analyzed, have the trainees teach the skills, addressing each step of the task analysis. Using a group of volunteers or other trainees for the instructor-in-training to teach will make this a fun and educational activity for all.

Have fun   *To clarify the skill of doing task analysis, bring a can of soda to class. Have the trainee/s guide you through each step it will take to open the can and take a sip. Follow their instructions very literally, taking nothing for granted. You will find this a fun and enlightening exercise for all.

Homework

Have the trainee/s observe a group of riders all performing the same skill. Have them identify the elements of the task that are most challenging for each rider. Next, discuss how he/she would assist each of the riders to be successful.

References:

Professional Association of Therapeutic Horsemanship International, *Instructor Educational Guide.*

Pony Club, *The Manual of Horsemanship*, International Printing House, Cairo, 1997.

Therapeutic Riding I & II Strategies for Instruction, 1998 ISBN 0-9633065-5-3, Editor Barbara T. Engel.

Task Analysis Worksheet

Level 1

Task: _____

Level 2

1. _____

1. _____
2. _____
3. _____
4. _____
5. _____
6. _____

2. _____

1. _____
2. _____
3. _____
4. _____
5. _____
6. _____

3. _____

1. _____
2. _____
3. _____
4. _____
5. _____
6. _____

4. _____

1. _____
2. _____
3. _____
4. _____
5. _____
6. _____

WHAT   SKILL PROGRESSION

WHY
By making our lessons progressive, we challenge our riders to improve. Each lesson should build on the last and be a bridge to the next. By identifying and building on our riders' accomplishments, we can increase confidence and help overcome weaknesses. By planning lessons that gradually increase in complexity and/or physical challenge, we bring our riders ever closer to the able-bodied riding experience. Over a session or a year, our effectiveness as instructors, our success, is defined by the progress of our riders.

The basic premise of Therapeutic Riding is that the learning of riding skills has therapeutic benefit. The rider's success in the arena translates to improved function in Activities of Daily Living (ADL). Progress and improvement are the primary goals for every student. The instructor's job is to prepare the riders to succeed, to benefit from every lesson.

HOW
Classroom

Pull the files on two or three of the students the trainee will be teaching. Review the long-term goals that have been established and plan objectives for a ten-lesson session. All ten objectives should address each rider's goals and be offered in a logical progression. All ten objectives should be riding skills that will progressively improve the student's skill level.

Have fun: *Brainstorm! Using the Semester Plan Form on the next page, choose a couple of riders with clear long-term goals, then start listing any and all riding skills that would address those goals. Once you have ten or twelve skills listed that are appropriate, sort them into a logical progression. How would you present them over the period of a ten-week semester? You're likely to have differing opinions on the order. None are wrong as long as they can be supported. (See attached form.)

<u>Homework</u>

Have the trainees list the goals of an entire class of three to four riders. Give them the time to take the list home and plan objectives for the entire group for a ten-week semester. This exercise now asks that the instructor plan a group goal and group objectives, as opposed to working with a single rider. This is a totally different skill and one that is essential for any Therapeutic Riding Instructor. We must teach a progressively challenging lesson to the strongest as well as the weakest rider in the group. We must find a way to benefit all.

References:

Professional Association of Therapeutic Horsemanship International, *Instructor Educational Guide.*

Therapeutic Riding I & II Strategies for Instruction, 1998 ISBN 0-9633065-5-3, Editor Barbara T. Engel.

Semester Plan – _____

(day/time/semester)

Riders _____

Goals _____

Skills/Activities:

_____   _____

_____   _____

_____   _____

_____   _____

_____   _____

Skill progression:

1) _____   2) _____

3) _____   4) _____

5) _____   6) _____

7) _____   8) _____

9) _____   10) _____

WHAT   PROGRESSION WITHIN THE LESSON

WHY   We prepare our riders to be successful in the objective—the skill to be taught that day—by including the following three steps in each lesson:

A) A **warm-up exercise**. It should be chosen with care, customized to be sure it will help the rider to accomplish the specific skill he or she will be asked to perform in the lesson.

B) We then focus on teaching the **riding skill** in depth. This is the objective of the lesson, with postural and positional corrections given to be sure the skill is learned correctly.

C) Once the skill is adequately reviewed, we offer an **activity** that allows the students to use the skill, to make it their own.

For example:

Warm-up	Riding Skill	Activity
Steering without reins—looking into turns; using eye, seat, and leg aids	Effective use of natural aids plus reins to weave poles	Pole-bending contest

HOW

Classroom

Using a flip chart or the Progression Within a Lesson Form included here, have the trainee/s call out four or five riding skills at random. Next to each skill, have them identify an effective warm-up exercise that would help a student become more successful in the skill. Write those down, too. Lastly, have them come up with an activity that would utilize the skill. If you type that chart up and give them each a copy, they will have a constant reminder of how to accomplish progression within the lesson.

Have fun

Challenge your trainee/s to list at least three warm-up exercises and three activities that would be appropriate for each riding skill listed. The next step would be to discuss which riders individually might most benefit from each of the choices. When working with groups of riders with varying ability levels, having more than one solution is always helpful.

Homework

Have the trainee/s expand their own list of riding skills with applicable warm-up exercises and activities. This will serve them well in years to come as they progress to teaching a wider variety of riders. We must teach a progressively challenging lesson to the strongest as well as the weakest rider in the group. We must find a way to benefit all.

References:

Therapeutic Riding I & II Strategies for Instruction, 1998 ISBN 0-9633065-5-3, Editor Barbara T. Engel.

Progression Within the Lesson

Exercise

Warm-up Exercise	Riding Skill	Activity

4

TEACHING TECHNIQUES

WHAT   TEACHING TECHNIQUES

WHY

There are techniques that can increase an instructor's effectiveness when teaching riders with disabilities. These include:

- Teaching to all **Learning Styles**

- Clearly expressing the **WHAT/HOW/WHY** of each skill

- Making **Postural and Positional Corrections**

- **Teaching to the Group**

- Utilizing good **Volunteer Management**

Because of their importance, each of these topics is covered separately in the following pages.

WHAT LEARNING STYLES

WHY

Each of us has a predominant style of learning. Some learn best from **auditory** input—the spoken or written word; others need a **visual** demonstration in order to grasp a concept or skill; still others require **kinesthetic or tactile** experience in order to learn. The ideal is to be able to learn through all three styles, but, particularly when working with riders with disabilities, this may not be the case. It is, therefore, imperative that a Therapeutic Riding Instructor have the skills necessary to teach to all three learning styles.

The majority of our students come to us eager to learn. If we present information in a style they cannot process, we not only limit their ability to progress, we may also create frustration, which can lead to lack of attention and behavior issues. It is our responsibility to discover how a rider learns, how best to communicate our instruction, and how to help them to be successful.

HOW

Classroom

- In the classroom, review the disabilities of the riders the trainee/s will be teaching. Review the characteristics of the disabilities to see if they determine a likely learning style. Next review a lesson plan for those particular students and discuss how the objective might best be presented/taught to accommodate the rider/s' needs.

| Have fun | Have trainees or volunteers simulate various disabilities. For example, one entire group could be deaf; another could be a group of blind riders; and a third group might have both disabilities. The trainee instructing will have to be creative to meet all of their needs and offer a lesson that is beneficial to all. |

Homework

Assign the trainee/s the task of reviewing all of their lessons to determine which learning style or combination of styles would be most effective for each group. Next, they will take the objective of their next lesson for those groups and decide how to best present it for those particular riders. Once they've taught the lesson, take time to discuss how effective they feel their instruction was and how the riders responded.

References:

Professional Association of Therapeutic Horsemanship International, *Instructor Educational Guide.*

Therapeutic Riding I & II Strategies for Instruction, 1998 ISBN 0-9633065-5-3, Editor Barbara T. Engel.

WHAT WHAT/HOW/WHY
COMMUNICATING THE OBJECTIVE

WHY

For a student to learn, an instructor must effectively communicate the riding skill, the objective of the lesson. To do so, an instructor must be able to convey the following information:

1) **What** is the riding skill to be learned? What will be expected of the student/s in this lesson?

2) **How** will they accomplish the skill correctly? What aids are required, what physical action is needed to perform the skill successfully?

3) **Why** is this skill worth learning? What incentive is there for the student/s to accomplish the objective?

This is the meat of a lesson. To be effective, an instructor must be able to explain the skill to be learned addressing all learning styles. Instructors must have the knowledge to teach the riding skill correctly and offer the needed corrections to guide their student/s to accomplish it successfully.

To truly learn the skill, the student/s must understand its application, how and when they will use it, and why. The explanations will have to be adapted to engage the particular rider/s being taught. A five-year-old is likely to respond to a very different type of explanation and incentive than an adult. An understanding of the rider/s and their very particular needs will dictate how a lesson is taught. This is the skill of teaching, what makes it so fascinating and fun!

HOW   <u>Classroom</u>

Have the trainee/s write a lesson plan. Have them then work on a script of how they will express the what/how/why of their planned lesson. Discussion should include the appropriateness of their explanations for the particular students they will be teaching. It will reflect their understanding of how to address the disabilities, as well as their level of knowledge of the skill to be taught. This is a wonderful exercise for evaluating the level of expertise your trainee has reached. It's a great guide for you as mentor to determine where you should place the focus in your next training sessions.

Have fun: **Once you've done an initial review of a lesson plan, have your trainee/s adapt their script for totally different riders learning the same riding skill. This is where creativity comes in! What adaptations are needed to effectively teach the same objective to two very different groups of people?**

<u>Homework</u>

Have your trainees observe experienced instructors. Have them identify how the instructor expresses—or fails to express—what/how/why in each lesson and how it is reflected in the success of the students. (See attached form to assist in the evaluations.)

<u>References:</u>

Professional Association of Therapeutic Horsemanship International, *Instructor Educational Guide 2002.*

Therapeutic Riding I & II Strategies for Instruction, 1998 ISBN 0-9633065-5-3, Editor Barbara T. Engel.

What/How/Why

As you observe this lesson, imagine yourself to be a PATH Certification Evaluator. List below any phrases you hear that answer the following questions:

What: What riding skill does the instructor want the student to perform? Is it clearly and thoroughly stated?

How: How should the student perform the skill? Listen for instruction/correction of posture and position and explanation of how to perform the skill correctly.

Why: Why is the instructor asking the student to do this task? Is there an explanation that might motivate the student to to master the skill?

What:

How:

Positional Corrections:

Postural Corrections:

Why:

WHAT   POSTURAL & POSITIONAL CORRECTIONS

WHY   Students do not come to us knowing how to perform riding skills, nor do they typically have correct posture and alignment. It is our job as instructors to teach these skills for their therapeutic value. Accomplishing them will afford the student improved functional levels in activities of daily living, as well.

Only by communicating to the rider *how* to accomplish a skill, or *how* to improve their posture, can they learn. Once we offer that information, we must then follow through and support their learning by observing their attempts and making corrections until they have accomplished the task successfully. Even if a student cannot attain truly correct posture and alignment, the closer they come to it, the greater will be their mobility and functional level. This is called approximation—coming as close as possible to the able-bodied ideal.

It may take months, it may take years, but the closer they come to correct posture and position, the greater their ability will become to perform everyday tasks. That is our goal for every rider.

HOW

Classroom

The classroom for this segment will be the arena. Have your trainee/s mount and discuss any terminology, phrasing, or imagery they have heard that was effective in their personal learning of riding skills. You can bet many of them will impact posture and alignment, as well as those that directly relate to riding skills, because correct posture and alignment are essential to being an effective rider. Let them demonstrate the difference the correction has made in their riding.

Next, ask them to consider which of their riders might benefit from the same correction; this might need to be communicated in a different way in order to accommodate a particular disability or learning style.

Have fun
It's your turn to get on a horse or stretching barrel. Strike postures and positions that are typical of your student population and let your trainee/s offer corrections. Be sure to respond as you feel their students will respond. Keep going until the needed corrections are made – it can take a while!

Homework

Assign each trainee three specific students to study/observe. Have them write at least three corrections they would offer to improve those riders' posture and alignment and three that would improve specifically their riding skills.

References:

Therapeutic Riding I & II Strategies for Instruction, 1998 ISBN 0-9633065-5-3, Editor Barbara T. Engel.

WHAT   TEACHING TO THE GROUP

WHY   Many of our riders have listed "improved socialization" as a personal goal. By offering the group-lesson setting, we offer them the opportunity to spend time with others in their age and/or ability level with a common interest and a shared experience. This gives them the basis for socialization in a positive setting and can yield great benefits. It also affords them a greater level of independence and decision-making than the one-on-one focus of a private lesson.

When there are two or more students in a lesson, each one should receive the benefit of the instruction. This increases safety as well as the efficacy of time spent in the saddle. Teaching to the group rather than focusing on one student at a time is a skill unto itself. It entails good arena management, a clear instructor's voice, a commanding arena presence, and solid lesson planning to maintain lesson flow. Riders should spend as little time as possible at the halt waiting for another rider to complete a task. Remember, it is the movement of the horse that is therapeutic! The instructor should be positioned to see all riders at all times to ensure their safety.

HOW

Classroom

Once again, the classroom is the arena. Have the trainee plan and teach to a group of three or four riders. Discuss the elements that impact the success of a group lesson, versus a private one:

- Arena layout—can the riders flow as a group?

- Instructor positioning—can all riders be seen at all times?

- Instructor voice—can the instructor be heard at all times?

- Effectively addressing each student's needs—is each given the needed input throughout the lesson?

- Rider spacing—are they close enough at all times for the instructor to see them consistently, but not too close for safety?

- Volunteer management—are volunteers used effectively as an extension of the instructor?

- Learning styles—is the instruction offered to address all learning styles so all can benefit?

Have fun

Invite a large group—at least five to ten—able-bodied riders to take part in a lesson. Place a Hula-hoop in the middle of the arena and tell the instructor they may not step outside the hoop. They must stay in the middle of the arena and effectively instruct all riders. This is an age-old exercise that is a bit extreme, but it does get the idea across that effective instruction *can* be offered to a large group of riders if the instructor is positioned to observe each and address each individually while the lesson flows.

Homework

Have the trainees experiment with equipment layout in the arena to see how the placement and spacing of ground poles, cones, and barrels can affect the flow of a group lesson. Circling a barrel before moving on to 2-pt. over poles that are a few feet away may work for one or even two riders, but this may cause a traffic jam with a group of three or four. It takes good planning to keep the class flowing.

References:

Therapeutic Riding I & II Strategies for Instruction, 1998 ISBN 0-9633065-5-3, Editor Barbara T. Engel.

WHAT VOLUNTEER MANAGEMENT

WHY
Volunteers are essential to a therapeutic riding program. If we had to hire people to lead and sidewalk with our riders, our fees would leap to unaffordable levels. Volunteers play a major role in the services we offer and their skill levels directly impact the quality of service we can provide. That skill level is determined by the quality of training we offer and the efficacy of the volunteer management employed by the instructor in the arena.

HOW
Classroom

Trainees should review the center's Volunteer Training Manual to be very clear on what they can expect from their volunteers. There should be consistency in how leaders are asked to hold a lead line or warm up a horse; there should be consistency in how sidewalkers are to be positioned and their role during different types of mounts and dismounts. Knowing the center's standards is essential to limit confusion in the arena.

Have fun
Have the trainee/s ride with a leader and two sidewalkers who have been coached before the class to do everything wrong – the leader can be just ambling along listlessly with the lead line in one hand or holding it so short that the horse can't move his head; the sidewalkers could be constantly talking to each other about their weekend or paying no attention to the rider at all while leaning all their weight on their arm on the rider's thigh. The sidewalkers could also be giving the "student" a riding lesson, making it difficult/impossible to follow both the sidewalker and the instructor. Of course they all came late for class as well, so the class couldn't possibly start on time.

This experience should drive home to the trainee just how important it is for an instructor to be aware of the impact volunteers can have on their riders and on the overall lesson.

Homework

Trainees typically have difficulty remembering that therapeutic riding is a team effort. If they have a background in able-bodied instruction, it is even more difficult to get comfortable with all those people in the arena! Reviewing each of their lessons and clarifying the role each volunteer should play, as well as how they can best benefit their rider, can give the trainee guidance on how best to direct their volunteers during class. They should keep in mind that the leaders' role is total focus on the horse; the sidewalkers' role is total focus on the rider. With a skillful leader and sidewalkers who perform as an extension of the instructor, the trainee should be able to step to the center of a group of riders and be free to teach to all while maintaining a consistent flow to the lesson.

References:

Professional Association of Therapeutic Horsemanship International, *Instructor Educational Guide* 2002.

Therapeutic Riding I & II Strategies for Instruction, 1998 ISBN 0-9633065-5-3, Editor Barbara T. Engel.

5

HORSEMANSHIP

WHAT   HORSE ANALYSIS

WHY

The type of horse that may be ideal for hippotherapy may differ from a horse that is ideal for vaulting, driving, or therapeutic horseback riding. The height and width of the horse, the type of movement, even the personality of the horse are all important elements that can impact the rider. It is an instructor's responsibility to match horse and rider to provide the greatest benefit.

For example: A student with Spastic Cerebral Palsy may require a narrow-based horse with smooth, fluid movement to reduce muscle tone, while a rider with Down Syndrome might benefit far more from a wide-based horse that would be less challenging to their balance, but with a trappy gait to increase muscle tone. The rider's body type must also be considered. Putting a person with a very narrow pelvis on a wide horse will result in posterior tilt; putting a person with a wide pelvic base on a narrow-based horse will clearly challenge their balance—which may be the goal…or not!

An instructor must be able to identify the conformation and movement of the horse and understand how it will impact a rider in order to offer the greatest benefit to their students.

HOW   <u>Classroom</u>

Classroom discussion should cover the following:

1. **Types of movement that will be of benefit to the rider and why:**

    Anterior/posterior tilt

    Lateral shift

    Rotation

    Smooth/fluid gaits

    Trappy gaits with more input

2. **What influences the movement of the horse:**

    Conformation

    Soundness

    Training

    Fitness

    Tack fit and adjustment

    Volunteer skill level (particularly the leader)

    Leading, lunging, long lining, or independent

    Collection or extension

    Activities within a lesson

3. **How the movement of the horse affects the rider:**

In other words, what makes riding therapeutic?

Have fun

Choose two or three horses with different types of movement—one with anterior/posterior; one with more lateral shift; one that provides full rotation. Mount able-bodied riders on each on bareback pads without reins (obviously, leaders will be needed). Place large colored dots or pieces of tape on the riders' backs at each shoulder and hip and on the horse, on each side at the slant of the rump. Have the trainee/s observe the movement in the rider as the horses walk directly away from them, and note whether they see more anterior/posterior action, more lateral or rotational. Is the horse's hip action symmetrical or do they drop one hip lower than the other? How does this affect the rider? The trainee/s can then mount and see if they feel the same input.

This is also a great opportunity to illustrate the effect a leader can have on a horse's movement. Have the leader tighten up on the lead line, holding it just below the horse's head, restricting movement; then have them slide the hand down twelve to eighteen inches, allowing the horse to move its head freely. The difference should be quite obvious. Also, try having the leaders march smartly forward, looking ahead versus dragging their feet, looking down at the ground or at the horse. This exercise can make a great impression that will inspire the trainee/s to take volunteer training and management in class very seriously!

Homework

An instructor should ride every horse they will have in class. As they ride them, they should apply what they have learned by noting which horse would be most appropriate/beneficial for each of their riders. This assessment should include not only conformation and movement, but also temperament, balance, and responsiveness to aids.

References:

Harris, Susan E., *Horse Balance, Gaits and Movement*, Wiley Publishing, Inc., Hoboken, NJ 1993.

Professional Association of Therapeutic Horsemanship International, *Instructor Educational Guide*.

Pony Club, *The Manual of Horsemanship*, International Printing House, Cairo, 1997.

Certified Horsemanship Association, *Horsemanship Manual*, 2008.

Evans, J. Warren, *The Horse*, Macmillan Publishing, 3rd edition,

Therapeutic Riding I & II Strategies for Instruction, 1998 ISBN 0-9633065-5-3, Editor Barbara T. Engel.

WHAT   HORSEMANSHIP SKILLS

WHY

An instructor is responsible for choosing appropriate horses for their program and for maintaining their health, safety, training, and overall welfare once they are part of the team. They are also responsible for the safety of their students while mounted in the arena. This requires an understanding of horse behavior, the ability to anticipate problems before they occur; and the ability to respond instinctively, properly, and effectively when they do. Knowledge of proper horse care and handling techniques is, therefore, imperative.

Horsemanship skills cannot be taught in a matter of weeks or months. Hopefully our trainees come to us with a background in horsemanship. If not, it is only fair to advise them that their training will be long-term. If your program cannot accommodate this type of training, it would be prudent to have a list of local barns available where they could work on their horsemanship skills and then return to pursue a career in TR. You might remind them that PATH Certification is RIDING INSTRUCTOR certification. They must first have the skills to be a riding instructor to then be able to apply them to working with riders with disabilities.

HOW   <u>Classroom</u>

An understanding and care of the horse covers a broad spectrum of knowledge.

Topics to be covered should include:

- Hay, feed, and supplements—types, nutritional benefits

- Recognizing unsoundness versus blemishes

- Footfalls at all gaits

- Ability to identify parts of the horse, markings, breed characteristics

- Ability to identify pulse, temperature, and respiration

- Bedding—types, pros and cons of each

- Stabling and turnout—options and benefits of each, maintenance

- Hoof care—trimming and shoeing options, how to maintain a healthy hoof

- Types and frequency of worming, dental care, and vaccinations

- Grooming—tools and benefits of each

- Basic care of wounds, illness, and unsoundness; when to call a vet

- Wraps—types and benefits of each

- Tack—types of bits and appropriate uses; types of saddle pads; types of girth; fit of tack; bridle versus sidepull versus halter use in class

- Schooling/conditioning – basic training and maintenance practices

- Handling techniques—working with the skittish horse; correcting vices; introducing the horse to the mounting ramp; training volunteers in leading techniques; bathing the horse; proper techniques for haltering, etc.

- Basic understanding of horse behavior—ability to identify and anticipate behavior issues and how to address them before they become a health or safety issue; ability to understand how a horse thinks/senses the world around him

- Ability to keep a horse healthy mentally and emotionally as well as physically.

Have fun   Every trainee should take part in the care, training, and schooling of the program horses, handling them daily and getting to know their needs. To build on that bonding experience, assign each trainee a horse to be under their care. For at least two weeks, preferably one month, they will be responsible for grooming, bathing, schooling, training, and providing health care for that particular horse. Set goals for the horse to have accomplished by the end of that period of responsibility. These could be basic training goals (for example: will swap leads) or the reduction of a vice (for example: will no longer nip when girth is tightened) or health care (for example: will lose or gain weight/muscle). Meet each week to review progress made.

Homework

Review with each trainee their strengths and where they need improvement in the above areas. Assign a topic of study to be reviewed each week until all topics have been covered. For example, one week they could review bits and their uses; the next week it may be an unsoundness they were not familiar with and how to care for it; or they may need hands-on practice of various wrapping techniques. Take it step by step until all topics have been covered.

References:

Harris, Susan E., *Horse Balance, Gaits and Movement*, Wiley Publishing, Inc. 1993.

Professional Association of Therapeutic Horsemanship International, *Instructor Educational Guide.*

Pony Club, *The Manual of Horsemanship*, International Printing House, Cairo, 1997.

Certified Horsemanship Association, *Horsemanship Manual*, 2008.

Evans, J. Warren, *The Horse*, Macmillan Publishing, 3rd edition.

Therapeutic Riding I & II Strategies for Instruction, 1998 ISBN 0-9633065-5-3, Editor Barbara T. Engel.

WHAT   PATH Intl RIDING DEMONSTRATION

WHY   PATH Therapeutic Riding Instructor Certification is awarded to those who demonstrate sufficient skills and knowledge to teach a basic riding lesson to people with disabilities. To be a riding instructor, one must have practical riding skills. The pattern PATH requires for the Registered Level is simply a tool that allows the evaluators to see that the candidate understands balance, movement, and appropriate use of aids. In the testing situation, the trainee will not be judged on how well they know the pattern, but on how well they ride each element.

To ride the pattern fluently requires knowledge of how to balance a horse both on the straightaway and on turns; how to bend a horse through circles and corners; and how to accomplish smooth upward and downward transitions from gait to gait. The rider must know and demonstrate correct diagonals at the posting trot and correct leads at the canter. All must be accomplished with a secure, balanced seat, with tactful rein and leg aids, and maintaining consistent control of the horse and consistent posture and alignment throughout. These are the key elements a riding instructor must be able to pass on to their students.

The candidate needn't be an Olympic-level rider to pass this test. They must, however, show sufficient skill to give the evaluators confidence that they could sit the trot without stirrups or perform any of the skills listed in the Registered Level criteria.

HOW

<u>Classroom</u>

Video-record the candidate/s riding the required pattern, then review the tapes in the classroom. Pay particular attention to the transitions. To accomplish smooth transitions, the rider must have a secure and effective position, must demonstrate an effective use of aids, and must convey an understanding of what they are requesting of the horse.

Have fun

Have the candidates *teach* the pattern to each other or to other able-bodied riders. By teaching the required skills, they will be made more aware of how to ride the pattern correctly, as well as place themselves in the position of the evaluators. It's a great exercise before going for certification testing.

<u>Homework</u>

Homework will depend on the strengths and weaknesses of each trainee. Some may need additional time in the saddle, others may need to ride a variety of horses, and another may need to simply learn the test.

<u>References:</u>

PATH Intl Registered Level Application Booklet—Certification Criteria..

Pony Club, *The Manual of Horsemanship*, International Printing House, Cairo, 1997.

Certified Horsemanship Association, *Horsemanship Manual*, 2008.

WHAT TACK & ADAPTIVE EQUIPMENT

WHY

Because we work with riders with disabilities, the tack we choose can make the difference between an unreasonable challenge and success. Assigning a flat, close-contact hunt seat saddle for the first ride of a student with Down Syndrome will probably not give them much confidence in this new situation. On the other hand, a nice, deep Western saddle or a deep-seated Dressage saddle could help them feel more secure, aid their balance, and therefore create a better environment for initial learning and success. As that rider progresses, that hunt–seat saddle might be the ideal tool to further challenge their balance and increase their tone.

We have many choices of tack. Understanding how each will affect our rider/s is one of an instructor's primary responsibilities. If we consider the purpose for which each type of equipment was designed, it can be very helpful in making those choices—do we assist the rider or do we challenge them? (See attached Tack Review for some examples.)

Proper fit of tack to both horse and rider is of utmost importance in choosing tack. A saddle or surcingle that does not fit a horse properly will cause discomfort and can lead to poor movement as well as behavioral issues. Tack that does not fit a rider properly will do the same. Because our horses can gain or lose muscle as well as weight over time, tack should be refitted at least annually. Having a professional review saddle fit is a great idea. Fit to the rider must also be reviewed on a regular basis. The Pony Club *Manual of Horsemanship* is a very helpful guide for fitting tack.

To allow our riders to progress in their riding skills, it may be necessary to adapt traditional equipment to accommodate their disability—whether it be paralysis; loss of a limb; lack of sensation in a limb; the inability to grasp a rein; spasticity; etc. A thorough understanding of the disability and how an adaptation will function is imperative, and a priority must be placed on *safety* for all concerned. An adaptation should never tie a rider to a horse, nor should it cause discomfort for horse or rider. (For some examples of adapted equipment, see attached Tack Review.)

HOW

Classroom

Spend some time reviewing the tack currently being used for your riders. Discuss other options: How they might influence the rider, for better or worse?

Have fun

An instructor should ride in the tack they plan to teach in, particularly if an adaptation is being used. By trying out that surcingle or adapted reins, they may discover better choices for their students!

Homework

Have the trainee/s switch their riders to different tack: If they usually ride English, have them ride Western, and vice versa. Any class can benefit from a bareback pad and surcingle lesson. Have the trainee discuss the impact the change of tack had on their students.

References:

Professional Association of Therapeutic Horsemanship International, *Instructor Educational Guide*

Pony Club, *The Manual of Horsemanship*, International Printing House, Cairo, 1997.

Certified Horsemanship Association, *Horsemanship Manual*, 2008.

Evans, J. Warren, *The Horse*, Macmillan Publishing, 3rd edition.

Therapeutic Riding I & II Strategies for Instruction, 1998 ISBN 0-9633065-5-3, Editor Barbara T. Engel.

TACK REVIEW

English saddles

The **Hunt Seat saddle** was designed to allow the horse freedom of movement over jumps, while galloping across the field, etc. The rider, therefore, is positioned for lightness in the saddle. Knee pads are positioned for a definite bend at the knee, hip, and ankle; the seat ranges from almost flat or close-contact, to only moderate support. The rider must carry their own weight and will get little assistance with balance.

The **Dressage saddle**, on the other hand, was created to afford the rider a very deep seat, to more effectively and tactfully influence the horse's balance and movement with subtle weight shifts and leg pressure during work on the flat. The proportions of the saddle ask for a longer leg, and a more open knee and hip to reach the leg down along the horse's sides to give subtle cues. The higher cantle and pommel provide more support than the hunt-seat, with a tendency to shift the pelvis toward anterior tilt.

The **All-Purpose saddle** is right between the two above. It is designed for a definite bend in the hip and knee, but not as deep as the Hunt Seat saddle. The seat is a bit deeper, but it is not as secure as the Dressage.

Western saddles

In general, the **Western saddle** was designed for the ranchman to ride all day. With a deeper seat, higher cantle, and swell, it allows the rider more security and relaxed comfort than the typical English saddle. There are, however, variations among the Western saddles, as well:

The **cutting saddle** is designed to help the rider keep their weight shifted back and down. This allows the rider to maintain balance while the horse is shifting positions and moving quickly to follow the cow. The deep seat, long leg position and high swell keep the rider deep in the saddle, while weight is shifted toward the cantle, the leg a bit in front of the hip, encouraging posterior tilt.

The **roping saddle** has almost the opposite function. While it is designed for the comfort of the rider, it encourages riding toward the front of the saddle and even lifting up out of the saddle to rope the cow.

The **trail or pleasure saddle** offers the rider support with a more balanced seat.

Surcingles

The surcingle, used with a thick Western or bareback pad, places the rider directly on the horse, allowing them to feel the warmth of the animal and transferring pure movement without other influences. Because the rider sits directly on the horse, with no lift from the saddle, the hip is spread wider, which may encourage posterior tilt, depending on your rider's conformation. There are also a variety of surcingles available:

The **one-handled surcingle** will bring the hands and, therefore, the shoulders to the center. The handle can be high or low, which again influences the position of the upper trunk.

The **two-handled surcingle** opens the shoulder girdle, offering a bit less support for the upper trunk, but typically positioning it in better alignment.

Surcingles, when used properly, allow a rider to push back away from the handle to stabilize a weak upper trunk. They can also give a sense of security to a new or very young rider. They allow freedom of movement for the rider working on vaulting or developmental positions or simply "around-the-world" exercises. Caution should be used to avoid leaning undue weight directly down on the surcingle, which can cause the horse discomfort and eventually soreness behind the withers.

ADAPTIVE EQUIPMENT

PATH standards must be followed when designing adaptive equipment. Such equipment should never secure the rider to the horse and should do no harm to the rider, the horse, or the volunteers. An instructor should always ride in the adaptive equipment first before putting their rider on board. This can give a greater understanding of how their student will function, as well as reveal issues not initially considered. Many adaptations, particularly those that reposition the spine or impact posture and alignment, should also be reviewed by a therapist before use. There are, however, many options that do not require approval:

Adaptive reins: Just about any type of material can be utilized to assist a rider's grasp of the reins. Experimenting with different textures; attaching bean bags to widen the grip; sliding bike grips onto the reins; bar reins; loop reins; a rein handle to assist the rider who can utilize only one hand—all of these are acceptable adaptations that can greatly increase a rider's independence.

Stirrups: As with all equipment, PATH Intl and program policies for the use of safety stirrups must be adhered to at all times.

Simply shortening or lengthening stirrups can have a dramatic effect on posture and alignment. Because the femur attaches to the pelvis, the opening or closing of the hip joint will encourage either anterior or posterior tilt. Caution should be used to adjust stirrups for the rider's maximum benefit; experimenting with different lengths might yield some welcome surprises!

For the rider who does not have control of any portion of the leg, the stirrups can be stabilized to a great extent without attaching the leg to the saddle. Using a long rubber band, place it first over the toe of the rider's boot, bring it back under the stirrup and give it a twist, then extend it back over the heel of the boot, preferably up to a spur rest or some protuberance that will keep it in place. You've now secured the foot to the stirrup in a way that will release itself should the rider fall. Lighter weight riders will require a lighter weight rubber band to be sure it will release properly.

Using yarn, a shoelace, or a dog collar, pass one end through the stirrup leather to tie the back of the leather to the girth. This will help stabilize the stirrup without attaching to the rider in any way. Be sure the leg hangs vertically once tied in place. This technique has been approved by the USDF as well as the Paralympic Committee for use at shows and can dramatically improve a rider's leg position and stability.

WHAT   Instructor-in-Training Review Form

WHY   To keep track of the topics covered with each trainee, it is helpful to record when the information is initially reviewed and when the trainee accomplishes an acceptable level of skill in the topic. By filling out the attached form, both you and your trainee will have a record of their progress, as well as what is yet to be reviewed.

HOW   Using the attached form, enter either a date of the initial review of each topic or a score from 1 to 3 reflecting the trainee's skill level. Once they have accomplished an acceptable skill level, you can again record either a date or a score (which should be a 3!).

Instructor-in-Training Review

Name: _____

	Initial Review (date and/or score)	Accomplished (date and/or score)
Registered Level Criteria		
Disabilities		
Posture & Alignment		
Mount & Dismount		
Lesson Plans		
Teaching Techniques		
Horse Analysis		
Horsemanship Skills		
Riding Demo		
Tack Review		
Volunteer Management		

The Mentor's Guide

References

Certified Horsemanship Association, *Horsemanship Manual*, 2008.

Evans, J. Warren, *The Horse*, Macmillan Publishing, 3rd edition.

Harris, Susan E., *Horse Balance, Gaits and Movement*, Wiley Publishing, Inc. 1993.

Kapit, Wynn & Elson, Lawrence, *The Anatomy Coloring Book*, Pearson Education Limited, England 2014.

Professional Association of Therapeutic Horsemanship International, *Instructor Educational Guide.*

Professional Association of Therapeutic Horsemanship International—*Certification Application Booklet— Registered Level.*

Professional Association of Therapeutic Horsemanship International, *PATH Intl Standards Manual.* Precautions & Contraindications.

Pony Club, *The Manual of Horsemanship*, International Printing House, Cairo, 1997.

Therapeutic Riding I & II Strategies for Instruction, 1998 ISBN 0-9633065-5-3, Editor Barbara T. Engel.

CPSIA information can be obtained
at www.ICGtesting.com
Printed in the USA
FSOW03n2055090616
21371FS

9 781457 538537